Blissful Leadership

A PATH TO INNER PEACE, JOY, AND FREEDOM

JANETTE BLISSETT

BLISSFUL LEADERSHIP:

A Path to Inner Peace, Joy, and Freedom

Copyright © 2021 Janette Blissett

ISBN: 978-8-743-73859-5
Author: Janette Blissett
Consultant: Brenda J. Young, PhD
Cover Design: The Purple Tape Studio
Photography: Posh Creative, Nancy Miller
Layout: Daniel Pierre
Publisher: Next Chapter Experience, LLC

ALL RIGHTS RESERVED

This book contains material protected under International and Federal Copyright Laws and Treaties. Any unauthorized reprint or use of this material is prohibited. No part of this book may be reproduced or transmitted in any form or by any means, electronic or mechanical, including photocopying, recording, or by any information storage and retrieval system without express written permission from the author at thenextchapterexperience@gmail.com.

The lotus flower is regarded in many different cultures as a symbol of enlightenment, self-generation, resilience, and rebirth.

Testimonials

"Leadership boils down to more than just style. Leadership is a commitment to observation and fundamental empathy. Janette is an intuitive creative and can identify self-proclaimed roadblocks. She will empower you to see past them with direct and practical solutions. Her abilities are uniquely applicable to those of us who want to be seen, heard, and activated. Janette will cut through the BS facade you may think you need to move forward. Instead, she will free you of those beliefs to maximize what makes you the most valuable player on anyone's team, not to mention your own."
—Daniel Pierre, The Purple Tape Studio

"By no means is this book a surprise to me. I have always known subliminally that there was a coach and leader within Janette. During our college years, before major exams, I would often experience sweaty palms. Knowing that words matter, she always managed to speak to exactly what I needed to hear and gave me the confidence I needed to get through it. Additionally, after class, she would be waiting for me to support whatever I felt the outcome was—pass or fail! Janette possesses a true gift, and after four decades of friendship, she still has it."
—Jackie Lawson, Retired Manager, SBM Life Science/Bayer Crop Science

"I am thrilled to see the unique leadership wisdom and energy that JB brings will be shared with a wider audience. In my work with her over several years, I have seen how she has left an indelible impression on those she leads and counsels. Janette has a keen ability to cut through superfluous nonsense and get to the heart of the matter that each individual person needs to hear. Her words are memorable, directive, and sincere. I have heard numerous people repeat phrases and guiding concepts that came directly from Janette months and years after her association with them. JB positively impacted my trajectory and outlook based on her caring support and encouragement. Those who follow her will enjoy her style and charisma and will also gain a deep respect that these lessons come from powerful experiences and courageous resilience."
—Glen White, CLU

"It wasn't until twenty-five plus years into corporate employment that I, for the first time, became a member of a highly effective team. What was different? I was now under Janette's leadership, which was a culture built on trust, loyalty, and integrity. We were encouraged to communicate often and knew that we always had Janette's ear and could seek her wisdom. We were allowed to create our own identity and told to, 'Just do the darn thing,' which we all came to understand meant to move forward and know that we

had Janette's support in success, and at times when things didn't go as well. If we needed to adjust, we would, but we always did what was right, what made sense, and what was in the customer's best interest. As important as her ability to maximize her talent, was her ability to make us laugh and enjoy what we were doing."
—Bob Bauer, Learning & Development Analyst

"Janette is an outstanding coach and leader who commits herself to the success of every person. She knows how to strike the perfect balance between challenge and encouragement. She also knows how to break down complicated things, so each person can focus on what is simplest and most vital."
—John Zimmerman, MAORL, CLU, ChFC

"As I thought about the time I was part of Janette's team, I came to realize that it wasn't the work I did that I enjoyed so much; rather, it was Janette's leadership that made me love my job! Janette empowered me to make decisions, trusted my judgment, had my back when I failed, and above all, inspired me to perform to my fullest potential."
—Marlisse Gonzales MBA, CLU, ChFC

"A leader of leaders and successful business owners, Janette Blissett is one of the greatest inspirations anyone could ever ask for. Janette's mastery of positive, uplifted realities is unparalleled. She effectively communicates how to emulate success principles in business and in life."

—Bruce Strothers, JD, Insurance and Financial Services

To my mother, Joyce Blissett, who possesses the heart of a lion, inspires me to believe in myself, and encourages me to be "scope-a-matic," embrace the future with a positive outlook, and pursue my dreams.

Table of Contents

Foreword 1

Introduction 3

Chapter One: Mindset Matters 7

Chapter Two: Blissful Leadership 17

Chapter Three: The Balancing Act 23

Chapter Four: Mindful Leadership 32

Chapter Five: Virtual Leadership 40

Chapter Six: Multicultural Leadership 48

Chapter Seven: How Are You Showing Up? 59

Conclusion 71

Foreword

Great leaders don't tell you what to do; they show you how it's done. I hope you are as excited as I am about this leadership book by Janette Blissett.

Let me give you a little of my background before I share my thoughts about the author. I worked for a Fortune 500, top 30 organization for thirty-three years, many of those in an executive leadership position. I was fortunate to have hired and trained hundreds of people who went on to key leadership positions in the company.

Janette Blissett was the first person I hired when I went into management.

When I meet and interview someone, my first thoughts are: "What could they achieve? Do they have a growth mindset?" Some people are born with natural abilities, while others have an inner need to grow, get better, and achieve more in their personal and professional lives. I then ask, "Does this person need motivation, or are they self-motivated? Can they see how individual growth can transfer positivity to their staff to help achieve peak performance in their business and personal lives? Do they understand that as the business role they are in grows, so does the person's role and responsibility?" I knew from the very beginning Janette could translate her vision and opportunity into reality. She took her initial opportunity and improved her skills and business knowledge over thirty years. I watched her move to key leadership positions, share her vision, and impact many people under her responsibility.

You will gain tremendous insight from Janette on her observations about the responsibility of the role of a leader. Each chapter will be a learning experience. I know the book will empower you, and what she shares in the book will provide the inspiration into "what's possible."

"The function of a leader is to produce more leaders, not more followers."
—Author Unknown

Best regards,

Michael Dannewitz
Retired Vice President
State Farm Insurance Companies

Introduction

I learned very early in life that my mindset is the one thing that controls my perceptions, what I think about, and what actions I take. My life from childhood through adulthood had been filled with experiences that gave me the ability to apply the superpower of my mindset to the things that mattered most to me. For example, setting my sights on winning the Martha Shapiro Award for high achievement in elementary school was one, and in high school, enrolling in night school to earn math credits qualifying me for an academic scholarship to attend Drexel University. All of those early experiences formed my mindset and gave me the ability to set a goal, focus, and achieve it.

Growing up in a Bronx, New York, housing project in a single-parent Caribbean home, what we lacked in resources we made up for in other ways. Those ways included all of the wonderful traditions we created around birthdays, holidays, and other events throughout the year. I recall how we meticulously prepared our apartment for when guests would arrive for Thanksgiving dinner. A few days before Christmas, I remember the entire family walking for blocks to the designated tree lot to buy a tree at the best possible price. And if it happened to be the scrawniest tree, we proudly carried the tree home and delighted in decorating it while having lots of laughs along the way. On hot summer days, someone would often open a fire hydrant, which we excitedly ran through to cool off, and the Fourth of July consisted of fireworks, sparklers, and kosher hot dogs. We always looked forward to Mommy's cake and ice cream celebrations for our birthdays. I fondly recall our back-to-school tradition of making sure everything was spic and span, clothes laid out, school supplies and book bags packed, as we anxiously awaited the first day of school. As simple as all of this may seem, those days fill me with gratitude, optimism, hope, and an appreciation for the simplest moments that make life great.

Moving on from Drexel University to Corporate America in sales management was a whole new world to which I had to adapt. Learning to maneuver through this environment with all its hierarchies and protocols became an interesting journey. Like bookends, I began and ended my career in the corporate arena. Sandwiched in between were extended times as an entrepreneur.

Now, in the second decade of a new century, the changing demographics of the workforce, where we work, and how we work demand we rethink traditional approaches to leadership. What may have been acceptable years ago is not acceptable now. The leadership playbook of old should be replaced with one that reflects multicultural diversity, authenticity, vulnerability, and a growth mindset. Also, leaders must not only just talk about it, but sincerely be about it as well.

Such leaders have the opportunity to influence and shape the outlook of the people they serve. Their teams depend on them to provide value-driven clarity on vision, purpose, and expected outcomes. In addition, employees want their leaders to be interested in them as people. To do that, leaders must be open to engage and be in touch with their people to get a sense of who they are beyond the job.

My best working relationships with leaders were with those who could authentically engage. I trusted and respected those leaders more than the others who were either egocentric, transactional, oblivious to the value of personally engaging, or simply lacked the skill set.

I hope this book will enable you to view leadership through a different lens, empower you to enhance your abilities through more profound reflection, and find balance in your life that will enable you to experience the joy of being a Blissful Leader.

Blissfully,
Janette Blissett

"This experience taught me that I was capable of taking a risk, being challenged but committed to it, and being transparent and vulnerable while in full view."

Chapter One

MINDSET MATTERS

A defining moment is a point in your life when you are urged to make a pivotal decision or when you experience something that fundamentally changes you. Such an experience occurred during a visit to Miraval Resort's Life in Balance Spa in Catalina, a community outside of Tucson, Arizona, where I undertook a challenge called Out on a Limb. In this challenge, I had to climb a telephone pole, walk across a log, and reach the other side. I thought to myself, this doesn't seem that hard to do. Little did I know the climb would be the easiest part. Getting to the starting point to begin the walk across the log suspended twenty-five feet in the desert sky is when the challenge really began. Reality and panic set in. Can I actually do this? Self-doubt began to set in. It was gut-check time.

To make it across, I had to let go of the pole, find my balance, and begin the journey across, one step at a time. Easier said than done because I was scared beyond belief. It seemed like an eternity before I managed to release that pole and begin "The Walk." I had five or six false starts, thinking I was ready, but then fear and panic would rise within me. I'd retreat back to the pole, where I felt safe. I forgot to mention I had an audience watching who had already made "The Walk" and were shouting words of encouragement.

I heard my friend, DeLynn, shout, "Don't even think about it. It's okay to take your time, Janette. You got this!" Enough time had passed. I had to let go of that pole. I had to prove to myself that I could do it. The time had come. It was now or never.

I silenced the voices of fear and doubt, steadied myself, released the pole, and took the first several steps forward. On every step, the only thing I told myself was breathe, breathe, breathe. I was about a third of the way when I said, loud enough for everyone to hear, "Okay!" It was like my mindset had shifted or rebooted. I was actually doing it. I heard another friend, Mercedes, shout, "Good job, Janette. You look like a ballerina. Keep on going!" Well, as you are probably thinking, I made it across that twenty-five-foot high log in the desert sky and immediately struck a triumphant pose when I reached the other side. I remember having a choice to disembark or walk across again. I chose the latter; however, this time, I had more confidence and no fear. This experience taught me that

I was capable of taking a risk, being challenged but committing to it, and being transparent and vulnerable while in full view. When I needed support, it was there, which I humbly accepted.

***

There was a point in my career when I felt uncertain about my future with the company. It may have been growing pains, but intuitively I knew something needed to change. So I reached out to my mentor, Mike D. to talk things out and gain perspective. During one of our mentoring sessions, he mentioned a professional coach he knew, Kathey, who he thought might be able to support me. I knew hiring a professional coach would be an investment in my personal growth, and I concluded it was worthwhile. Kathey and I hit it off at our first discovery meeting. She uncovered my backstory, my current state, my vision of the future, and the things I needed to gain clarity on. It is often said that to experience the mental or emotional shift needed to make progress, one has to do "the work." If I wanted to gain clarity, experience peace, joy, and fulfillment, I had to do "the work." So that's what I did.

As I began to make incremental changes in my personal life and experience noticeable and sustainable results, I became more optimistic about the present and future, and more self-assured and confident. I learned that I am willing to take calculated risks with an optimistic outlook even when the results could end in success or failure, to learn from the experience, and to appreciate those teachable moments. With this mindset, I increased my self-confidence, became more adaptable, responded well to change, and had clarity on the future. My transformation had an overarching effect on how I related to my work, team, and business partners.

That was the beginning of my journey toward defining the things that mattered most in my personal and professional life. Very important to me and at the top of my list are quality of life and longevity. As my lifestyle choice, I made a decision to love myself to optimal health.

Committing to a regimen of self-care and wellness was my first order of business. I thought of it as a prudent investment with a major payoff in the now and in the future. After trial and error, starts and stops, I finally found a wellness program I loved and looked forward to and was sustainable for life. The results that were so hard to achieve in the past are now my reality. As others witnessed my transformation, it created the opportunity to mentor, inspire, educate, and support others as they adapt to this new mindset and lifestyle.

These personal experiences have confirmed that mindset prevails over everything I think about, say, and do. This mindset shift enabled me to find happiness in my personal life, joy in my work, and a sense of empowerment. It was freeing to find the balance I needed to be unafraid to lead with heart, embrace authenticity, and take risks. When I showed up as myself, the conversations transformed as well. They became more engaging, enjoyable, and profoundly genuine and always had a sense of positive energy and an expectation of reciprocal engagement.

Having an evolved mindset empowered me to objectively see situations for what they were, then think beyond or around obstacles when they occurred. Mastering the power of mindset and making it a focal point for my team enabled us to clearly focus our energies on the things that mattered. It's very easy to get stuck in a negative thinking cycle—no doubt about that. So we accepted the fact that it is normal to feel a certain way about things. We allowed ourselves to have our "moment" when the unexpected and sometimes ridiculous happened, developed a sense of humor about things that were not in our control, and then accepted the reality of the situation based on the circumstances. Applying this approach, my team and I agreed that shifting our focus and energy toward resolving issues instead of magnifying them was time and energy better spent.

Understanding these dynamics and being mindful in those moments triggered an immediate change or reset in our disposition, energy, and focus. This approach allowed me to provide support and direction to the team as we responded to critical situations. Also, it helped us keep our focus on the main thing. Critical conversations were easier to have as we built bridges of understanding and connection. The objective was to avoid going down an emotional rabbit hole and staying there too long, which in my opinion is a complete waste of time and energy. When our mindsets were open, optimistic, and positive, we were more productive, able to problem solve and manage situations more effectively and with greater ease. Team alignment, with everyone on the same wavelength, created great synergy, which we discovered was very evident to our peers, training associates, and business partners.

There were occasions when an executive leader was scheduled to drop in on one of our workshops. On one particular day, as scheduled, Milt attended. After observing the team in action during our morning session, he remarked that we were always so upbeat, positive, and highly energized every time he visited, which seemed to create a high level of engagement with our associates in training. He asked, "Why do you think that is, Janette?" I proudly replied without hesitation, "Mindset!" I was thrilled he recognized the difference it was making in the team and our performance, and its impact on our associates in the workshop.

***

When dealing with unanticipated situations, my experience has taught me to find balance through what I call the head and heart mindset. Knowing that sometimes the unexpected will inevitably happen, when it did, I simply took responsibility, handled the situation, learned from it, and kept the momentum going.

Here's an example illustrating how your mindset can set things in motion that you may not have intended. I was involved in a management meeting with a leader. I had become accustomed to his penchant for protocols and keeping everything status quo. He had a tendency to magnify unexpected issues or situations that arose with more of an emphasis on how it made him look rather than focusing on finding a solution. However, despite our differences in perspective, I decided it was best to have patience (head) and be open (heart) to whatever he had to say because he obviously thought it was very important. There was a point in the meeting where my calm demeanor may have come across as dismissive to him, which was not my intent. However,

I soon discovered he had anticipated a completely different reaction from me. Well, the meeting concluded, and we moved on to our next meeting. On the way there, I received a text message. At first, I didn't quite understand why I had received it. But I very quickly figured out the message was not meant for me. It was meant for someone who wasn't even involved in our meeting or discussion. The text recapped our meeting, and he expressed concern about my seeming lack of reaction. The fact is, having sent the text message in the first place was definitely counter to creating a culture of trust. It was meant for someone who wasn't even involved in our meeting or discussion. So when we continued on to our next meeting, I intentionally positioned myself across from him to read his body language. He appeared uncomfortable, and it seemed he couldn't make eye contact with me. I thought to myself, "He has some explaining to do. This is going to get interesting."

I knew a conversation was inevitable, but felt it was his responsibility as a leader to be accountable for what he put into motion, his mindset, and how he showed up. Well, he had a flight to catch immediately after the meeting and left saying he'd call me from the airport. When he did call, we exchanged pleasantries, and then finally the moment of truth arrived. He did the typical mea culpa, discussed how I came to receive the text, and offered an apology, which I graciously accepted. I asked several follow-up questions for clarity, reassurance, and understanding, then simply wished him well in his travels. In the end, I believe how I showed up and handled this situation defined my relationship with this individual from that point on. We all have missteps in life and have to take responsibility for them. I've had my share personally and professionally and have no shame in admitting that. As Maya Angelou said, the question to ask yourself is, "What is the lesson in this?" I certainly hope this leader has gained the wisdom to ask himself that question in the future.

Dr. Wayne Dyer once said, *"If you change the way you look at things, the things you look at change."* I embraced this philosophy and included it as foundational to my mindset growth.

"I needed to trust that the wisdom acquired from my life's journey could guide me, provide a sense of peace, and offer personal freedom."

Chapter Two

BLISSFUL LEADERSHIP

Within Blissful Leadership is a symbiotic relationship between your personal and business lives. It requires that you first begin by facing your realities, having a clear vision of who you are, who you want to become, and what matters most to you.

Taking ownership of outcomes in my personal and professional lives was a daunting task. Those two dynamics often appeared to be in direct conflict that threatened a sense of balance within me. I found that being out of balance when things aren't clear can cause overwhelm. When I am in alignment, the things that show up for me are those that serve me well. Blissful Leadership began with turning traditional boundaries into the source of my power and creativity and ended with me thriving in profound balance. I learned through introspection and reflection how to gain clarity on my absolutes and life vision. I considered the hard work it took to create the clarity I needed. Now, in retrospect, I marvel at the confidence I had to explore new opportunities leading to self-actualization and fulfillment. However, I still needed to trust that the wisdom acquired from my life's journey could guide me, provide a sense of peace, and offer personal freedom. I not only needed to determine where I was on the journey, but also consider what was possible.

***

Leaders who are decisive, engaging, adaptive, and reliable have had the most significant impact on my leadership development journey. In the early stages of my corporate career, an incredible mentor and leader came into my life. He was a great influence on both a professional and personal level. That alone speaks volumes about him as a leader and as a human being. Even after he retired and left the corporate world, I can still call Mike D. and his wife Karen very dear friends. There is an African proverb that says, "It sometimes takes a village." In my case, in addition to Mike, I am very fortunate to have had several others within and outside the company who I considered great leaders, mentors, and role models.

When I worked with several other new managers and leaders, I did find myself comparing them to their predecessors. This is probably customary when new leaders are introduced. It was easy to discern the difference in their leadership preferences, styles, and abilities. I am pleased to say many of them met my expectations; however, it was obvious to me when they missed the mark and seemed to be more interested and invested in themselves rather than developing their people.

What continued to disappoint me was that though these managers may have had moments of brilliance, they lacked the ability to move past just directing their people and getting the work done. I classified these types of leaders as transactional. They function purely as managers with little sense of or curiosity about who their people are beyond the work or how to support them. Their focus is on directing and controlling their team just to coordinate efforts toward accomplishing the business goal. It appeared they were quite satisfied with creating an echo chamber filled with employees who dutifully told them what they wanted to hear. Very few employees wanted to take the risk of rocking the boat or gaining a reputation for not being a team player. The practice of "going along to get along" or "just playing the game" is still very prevalent in many organizations.

Understanding the state of affairs with these transactional leaders who clearly had their agenda and being unwilling to be marginalized by them, I developed my own agenda. I became committed to investing in my personal development despite them. As a result, I expanded my view of leadership by intentionally creating mentoring relationships to fill the leadership gap I was experiencing. The leaders who mentored me were focused on leading their people. They had the ability to influence, motivate, and enable others to contribute toward the success of their stated goals.

With the mindset of appealing to the heart and head, it was evident to me that both approaches were necessary in a leadership position. I was determined to provide my team with a totally different experience from what they may have had with other leaders. One thing I wanted to avoid was exerting my power through position, title, or authority. Instead, my preference was to invest time and attention in my people, encourage, inspire, and influence them to show up ready for prime time. As I expanded my mindset, it created opportunities for reciprocal exchanges that were deeper and more personal. I opened up, and so did the team, as did many other people in my business and personal life.

Blissful Leadership emerges when you understand how the way you show up influences the perception and outlook of others around you and how they experience you. Very much like transformational leadership principles, Blissful Leadership builds on authenticity, vision, and creating an environment where employees are inspired and encouraged to work in their genius zones. When the "me" syndrome changes to a "we" mindset and you lead with confidence and heart, your people will see and appreciate the opportunity to do their best work. Once that mindset shift took place, it became a part of me, my brand, and eventually my legacy.

"Nothing is more important than reconnecting with your bliss. Nothing is as rich. Nothing is more real."
—Deepak Chopra

"The best leaders were skilled at balancing the head and heart of leadership. Being responsible for driving results through other people, these leaders understood the importance of relationship building."

Chapter Three

THE BALANCING ACT

Balancing technical skills with soft skills is key to effective leading. It is very apparent when a manager or leader has low emotional intelligence and lacks self-awareness. They sacrifice building relationships with their team members for a single focus on driving results and getting the job done. Many times, the result is a team that lacks engagement, enthusiasm, and connectivity.

During the course of my career, I concluded that the best leaders were skilled at balancing the heart and head of leadership. Being responsible for driving business results through other people, these leaders understood the importance of relationship building. Knowing that some team members were motivated by social recognition, awards, and incentives, they intuitively tailored their approaches in ways that appealed to each individual. We always knew what was at stake and the level of contribution expected from us. Going beyond what we thought was even possible and actually achieving it made us all more confident about our potential. Most of the time, the goals were lofty, and the challenges to reach them were real, but those leaders were still able to provide the right amount of encouragement and support to keep us optimistic and motivated.

I can name many examples of great leaders, but there is one who made a distinct impression very early in my career. I worked with an executive leader named Mike D, who put out a very challenging goal for our sales team. Mike's approach with us was simple and straightforward. He set the stage for us to weigh in based on our capacity, then challenged us to exceed what we thought was even possible. He helped us see the big picture as a win-win-win situation. Amazingly, the majority of us rallied around Mike and enthusiastically went after that goal.

We had days when we were on top of the world and filled with great confidence. Then there were other days when we were simply in the pits for myriad reasons. A few times, we questioned whether we had bitten off more than we could chew or even achieve. But Mike was there every step of the way, helping us combat self-doubt and building our confidence to keep us focused and in the game.

Mike's ability to meet us where we were, give us the space to emote without judgment, collaborate, and inspire us to push through our self-doubt meant the difference between success and failure. He saw us at our best and sometimes at our worst but never cast judgment about our abilities or even our potential. That spoke volumes about the leader Mike was.

That month our team exceeded the original goal and broke seven company sales records. Mike had what I called the Pied Piper effect. He suggested we travel to the regional office and drive in to deliver our business applications, which we were proud to do. We met early in the morning and traveled to Lincoln, Nebraska, caravan style, five cars deep, to receive recognition for a job well done and our promised rewards. I felt privileged to ride in Mike's car. We even stopped at the Copper Kettle Restaurant to grab a bite to eat on the way there. Good times inspired by an exceptional leader.

Another leader who made a major impression was Jeff, an example of a transformational and servant leader. It was motivating and inspirational to work in an environment where I knew I was being mentored, coached, and supported. He challenged and encouraged me to be solution oriented, leverage my ability to creatively problem solve, and focus on my personal development. While I was on Jeff's team, he helped me tap into and leverage the value of my education, experience, and expertise.

It was inspiring to get to know Jeff and work with him. Our conversations were varied, many, and quite engaging. Topics ranged from the business, family, and personal beliefs, to aspirations and our vision of the future. When my marriage was unraveling, leading to separation and eventually divorce, I felt comfortable sharing my concerns about attending a national company meeting at such a critical time in my life. Jeff said he completely understood. I appreciated the fact that he had the compassion to support me in my decision. Jeff handled the cancellation of my flight, hotel, and meeting reservations without hesitation, second-guessing, or having anyone else weigh in. I needed time to deal with my reality and contemplate what my new life was going to be. My shih tzu, Jadabear, was five years old at that time. I recall the moments we comforted each other. I cried on and off for about two weeks before deciding I was done. I was totally uninterested in looking back. Prepared emotionally to move on, I turned the page to begin a new chapter of my life.

The years spent under Jeff's leadership subtly shifted my outlook on leadership responsibility. Jeff was a leader who never claimed to have all the answers, encouraged us to explore creative solutions through collaborative and healthy debate, and challenged us to be innovative in our approach. Understanding that a high level of engagement and performance was expected of our team, Jeff was extremely resourceful and strategic. He provided us with the personnel and tools needed to accomplish our business goals. Sometimes we would marvel at how he consistently was able to pull out all the stops. Jeff made it look easy, but with the typical corporate BS involved in getting anything done, I'm quite sure it wasn't.

We could always count on Jeff to be supportive, firm, and honest with his feedback. Jeff's actions as a servant leader were fulfilled as he cultivated a culture of trust, fostered leadership in others, encouraged diversity of thought, and demonstrated a growth mindset.

With Jeff's coaching, I completed my second insurance designation through The American College. This helped position me as a competitive candidate for upcoming growth opportunities. As fate would have it, the company announced the development of a new department and the creation of four new teams. One of the hub locations for the new department was in Phoenix, Arizona, a place I had lived earlier in my career and one I had aspired to reside in again. I eagerly set my intention around being selected to lead the Phoenix team. Months seemed to crawl by at a snail's pace as business plans were firmed up and candidates were vetted. I remained optimistic, and I woke up every morning with the intention firmly planted in my mind. Several times throughout the day, a daily mantra reaffirmed that intention. I put it into the universe, put my head down, and continued to focus on doing the work. Then one evening, when I was traveling on company business, Jeff called to share the news. My focus, determination, perseverance, and hard work had paid off. I had been chosen for a position on the leadership team. Four months later, my shih tzu, Jadabear, and I were relocated to our new home in Phoenix, Arizona.

Not all leaders are cut from the same cloth. We realize they have strengths and their own opportunities for development. The problem is many simply lack emotional intelligence and self-awareness, which can be the kiss of death for any organization with leaders who have that gap. Unfortunately, most of these individuals think they are really leading and adding significant value, but their leadership gap causes the complete opposite effect in most cases. Under those circumstances, many employees become unmotivated to work enthusiastically or perform at their highest level, resulting in a no-win situation. If not checked or curtailed, these leaders end up alienating team members, losing their respect, and gaining an unflattering reputation over time.

I once worked with an executive leader for whom I initially had high expectations. I envisioned us developing a great working relationship and collaborating well to achieve planned business goals. At the beginning of our association, I called him one Saturday afternoon (as I had been invited to do by other executives I worked with in the past) and immediately knew it would be different working with him. It may have been bad timing on my part, but it was obvious he did not appreciate me initiating a call on a weekend. After that, I never did. This was unfortunate because deeper connections were developed in those impromptu moments in my experience with other executives. It may have been my uncertainty about our relationship that caused our conversations to be generally polite, cursory, and mostly business. The relationship with this leader always seemed one-sided, and it never fully blossomed as I had hoped. It wasn't easy to accept at first, but as I moved into other positions and worked with other leaders, I regained optimism for my future.

As another example, a former colleague shared he was working with a leader who, from his perspective, had created a very tenuous and negative work environment. Any attempt to gain clarity on work objectives or even offer input was met with resistance or flat out rejected. When he exercised the company's open-door policy, the response he got from a senior executive was, "Well, he's been around a long time and probably won't change." When I heard that, I shook my head in disappointment and asked myself, "Was that the best this so-called leader could do?" Sad to say, this scenario was a prime example of kicking the can down the road. Absolutely pathetic and mind-boggling, in my opinion, but it is a reality that there are leaders like this one who, for whatever reason, are allowed to fly under the radar.

"The responsibility of leadership is not to come up with all the ideas. The responsibility of leadership is to create an environment in which great ideas can thrive.
—Simon Sinek

"Cultivating an environment where team members are confident about sharing can be challenging if trust is not established. Trust is built by leaders who are tuned in and who purposefully listen."

Chapter Four

MINDFUL LEADERSHIP

Leadership always involves other people and is a two-way street. In the words of John Maxwell, "He who thinks he leads, but has no followers, is only taking a walk." What high-performing leaders intuitively know, and I learned over time, is that you have to listen and observe in order to develop your people effectively. Intuitive and intentional leaders have the expertise needed to assess the amount of leadership required to support their team's development and ability to execute company initiatives and goals. They recognize some team members may be at varying developmental stages and have different developmental needs. So they may need more definitive direction or guidelines at certain stages of their development. No one benefits when the blind are leading the blind, no doubt about that. The leader's job is to discern the team's capabilities and then determine the best leadership approach needed. Therefore, mindful leadership is always needed and appreciated.

***

Earlier in my career, I recall completing a company-wide 360-degree feedback survey for new managers. Based on the results, two executive leaders named Reid and Carra took an interest in my development and recommended I attend the Center for Creative Leadership (CCL) in San Diego, California. There was no judgment, simply a desire to see me grow into my potential. Many thanks to them for giving me that opportunity and providing the leadership and support I needed as I continued my development.

The results from the 360-degree feedback survey coupled with the Myers-Briggs Type Indicator (MBTI) were eye-opening. For several reasons, it was a very emotional time for me, and I was on the verge of tears most of the time at the CCL. As the time there came to an end, I instinctively knew I needed the courage to have several uncomfortable conversations with the team. Upon my return from CCL, my team and I engaged in several heartfelt dialogue sessions about the basis of their feedback and expectations on how we would move forward. With complete transparency, we developed a strong bond that allowed us to enjoy the process of learning about each other and appreciating our uniqueness as individuals. That experience was the beginning of my journey as a developing leader.

***

Cultivating an environment where team members are confident about sharing can be challenging if trust is not established first. Trust is built by leaders who are tuned in and who purposefully listen. The leaders who asked thought-provoking questions and took the time to listen were the ones I trusted, confided in, and worked with the best. They were also observant and able to provide substantive feedback that contributed to my growth.

All employees benefit from leaders who can inspire and motivate them to reach high-level objectives and support them through planning, coaching, and providing accountability measures. Interesting to note, these leaders were the most open-minded and secure enough to create an environment where "coaching up" was also accepted. I have had personal experience with receiving feedback from my team and know those times can be very humbling. But in those teachable moments, you learn a lot about yourself and the individuals you lead. Those are the moments when authentic connections are created.

With certain leaders, especially those new to the role, you may have to risk testing the waters to figure out how open they are to feedback. I had the occasion to do that with a leader who was scheduled to visit and spend time with the team. We were in the midst of facilitating a workshop for a very large group of associates and were energized by the challenge of keeping a high level of engagement. This leader was cordial when he arrived, but his body language indicated he had something else on his mind. Before long, he signaled that he wanted to talk. So we stepped out of the training room and found a place to meet. I was thinking, "This must really be important." It turned out he was upset about something and felt he had to address it. He shut down any attempt on my part to provide an explanation. I had no choice but to listen to his rantings. I was annoyed with his disruptive approach and mentally drew a line in the sand. I said to myself, "This is not over."

Deciding to stand on principle irrespective of protocol, the following day before our workshop began, I asked to meet with him. I shared my perspective about how he approached me, and with the table turned, it was now his teachable moment. A few years later, while having lunch, we talked and laughed about that incident. What's interesting is that his memory of it was completely different from mine. Apparently, that encounter left an indelible impression on him.

In my experience, one-dimensional leaders were always great at assessing and judging. I could have resorted to feeling frustrated and marginalized, but having a growth mindset helped me accept this reality as part of my journey. It enabled me to be resilient enough to maneuver through their dysfunction, learn through observation, and then create options and solutions that enabled me to thrive personally and professionally. Turning traditional boundaries or limitations into the source of my superpower became second nature and allowed me to push through even in the face of great odds. Fortunately, I had mentors, my coach, and a self-driven development plan that prepared me for other future opportunities.

***

Leaders are responsible for creating a work environment that is positive and motivating. However, some leaders create a dysfunctional, toxic, and demotivating climate. Unfortunately, many of these leaders perform publicly one way for the show, but create a completely different dynamic for their employees when out of plain sight. I've observed that there are many leaders who need the self-awareness to stop talking, stop sucking up all the air in the room, and stop blocking the creative genius of their team. They need to know that when all the talking is only from their perspective and the team is not giving input or providing feedback, there is a reason for that. Trust is established when team members have a sense of confidence that they have the opportunity to be heard, acknowledged, and taken seriously. Some managers and leaders create an environment where self-interest is their only priority.

It really is a shame because many employees are negatively impacted yet feel they have no recourse. In an attempt to gauge employees' perspectives on leadership, many organizations use surveys asking employees to give feedback. In actuality, although the surveys are deemed confidential, many employees are uncomfortable with telling it like it is for fear of retribution, or they doubt anything will ever change. Even when the open-door policy is used to inform the leadership of what is really going on, there is no guarantee anything will come of it. The system seems flawed, especially when things remain the same after concerns and grievances are expressed and exposed. Working in a dysfunctional or toxic environment can be debilitating for employees from a career and confidence standpoint, no matter how talented they are. However, with persistence and perseverance, optimistic employees decide to look for opportunities inside the company with the hope of having a better experience the next time around. Other employees who are frustrated and fed up leave their company for greener pastures. The reality is that many companies lose some of their best and brightest due to drawbacks in the system they have no idea is really not working.

Learning through experience and observation, I took a different approach with my team. I intentionally removed my ego, focused on providing clarity on the objectives, listened to feedback from those willing to give it, and empowered the team to apply their creative genius to drive business results. My mindful leadership style was the pathway to the bliss I experienced with my team. I'm quite sure you've heard the phrase, "Teamwork makes the dream work." Well, it's true.

"We are not a team because we work together. We are a team because we respect, trust, and care for each other."
—Vala Afshar

"Leaders who adapt quickly, are innovative, and learn new ways to stay in touch with their teams have the potential for a win-win. Adaptability has definitely become the new currency."

Chapter Five

VIRTUAL LEADERSHIP

The COVID-19 pandemic has caused a paradigm shift regarding how we work and how we lead. The business justification for embracing the virtual environment is a reality and more important now than ever before. Let's start by addressing one aspect of leadership that may not be talked about openly. To be specific, I call it *unconsciously leading from privilege*. Leading from a place of privilege is something leaders should be cognizant of and avoid at all costs. Simply put, leaders must be mindful and understand that not everyone has the same resources, home office setup, or environment as they may have. There needs to be awareness that spouses or life partners may be working together from home in close quarters while supporting children being home-schooled. Also, many employees working in less-than-ideal environments at home are also trying to balance other parallel priorities that can influence the typical work schedule. This is definitely an adjustment for everyone, not to mention the impact these demands may have on your team members' ability to perform at previous performance levels. This is not to say expectations should be lowered; however, leaders should develop more of a panoramic view of each team member's overall unique circumstances relative to their contributions.

In addition to accepting the fact that working with and providing leadership to teams in the virtual environment is here to stay, understanding that new rules will apply is also key. This new dynamic requires learning a new set of leadership skills. It has been noted that while people skills generally account for the majority of leader success, many leaders focus mostly on their technical skills, but so much more is expected and required to get the job done. People who lead virtual teams need to adopt special skills that include understanding the dynamics of maintaining interactions without the benefit of normal social cues from conversations that usually take place in face-to-face work environments.

To stay relevant in this new reality, leaders must have the ability to effectively use social networking and communication technology as their main means of communicating and collaborating, while maintaining a personal approach. Finding the balance can be challenging for hard-wired leaders who have a deep attachment to doing things the way they've always done them. The virtual environment requires managers and leaders to learn more effective techniques and decision-making strategies that create energy and sustain a high level of engagement. Managers and leaders must reboot their mindset in order to embrace this new reality. Virtual team members expect and benefit from leadership who support them with clarity, effective communication, responsiveness, and trust.

There are significant individual and team development opportunities in the virtual environment that leaders should not overlook. Clear goals and encouragement for team members to stay engaged and rely on their resources will give leaders insight into how individuals on the team approach their work. Career development conversations are necessary and expected even in the virtual space. Leaders can still rely on best practices used in face-to-face interactions, but will have to embrace doing it better and doing more in the virtual environment. It may be a different dynamic on the virtual platform, but there is an expectation for leaders to continue to focus on each team member's development.

It may feel quite transactional with the number of emails and Zoom meetings in the virtual space. However, well-timed touch-base calls with the team and individually can help leaders determine what support is needed, help create a roadmap for the team member from a growth standpoint, and keep everyone motivated and connected. Recognizing individual contributions, life events, and milestones will make each team member feel appreciated. Leaders should foster a virtual team community by celebrating team successes and helping them create relationships with others they can network with and go to for support. In my role as leader, I found having a creative communication strategy added a level of positive energy and made the interactions more enjoyable. Opening a window of time for the team to connect with me for impromptu conversations went a long way toward building confidence by being accessible, responsive, and supportive.

Many of my former colleagues and team members now working virtually have expressed frustration with leaders who over-utilize Skype and Zoom platforms without recognizing or considering their adverse effect on productivity. It should be noted that very few employees enjoy being on virtual calls or meetings from 7:30 a.m. to 6:00 p.m. If they do, they are in the minority. So, leaders, please do not use this approach if you expect to earn your team's confidence. They will humor you by being compliant, but that will be as good as it gets.

What they also shared as a concern was the tendency of insecure leaders to either micromanage or overload the workday in an attempt to ensure everyone is working at full capacity. Overtly attempting to micromanage virtual teams is counterproductive, ridiculous, and insulting. Leaders with this proclivity need a major mindset reboot. Their focus should be on communicating the expectations to ensure everyone is on the same page. If the work is getting done and meets set expectations, then call it a productive day. When goals are met, there should not be a concern about how and when a person is working. Remember, virtual leadership is an entirely different dynamic. With employees working from home, they may be overseeing their children's educational needs and family realities as well as attempting to find a balance to fulfill their job responsibilities.

In the past, I've worked with leaders who displayed a lack of trust when their team members worked remotely from home. Out of curiosity, I asked what their concerns were with that arrangement. The response was never definitive. However, from my perspective, this was a serious trust issue. There was a pervasive belief that employees couldn't possibly be as productive working from home as they could be when working in the office.

To gain additional perspective, I asked several team members their opinions. They shared that the open floor plan concept the company adopted provided little to no privacy. It created the opportunity for a multitude of interruptions throughout the day. Oftentimes when the team did come to the office, they would set up in any unoccupied work area just to have privacy and uninterrupted time to make calls, do project work, or simply get assignments done. From their perspective, the only real reason to go into the office is to attend planning meetings, training workshops, and meetings with business partners or leadership.

There were many elements I considered that supported working virtually on some days. First, we avoided the daily grind and hassle of drive time and traffic delays going to and from the office. Second, we all were able to reallocate that drive time and instead use it to drive results in our areas of responsibility or engage in self-development activities to expand our knowledge base. Third, the quality of our work demonstrated we were high performers with a high sense of accountability for our work product.

For all the energy spent on second-guessing the efficacy of working virtually—reality check—it is now the new normal, and many employees have adapted well to this new virtual dynamic. The paradigm has shifted, and virtual work environments are the new normal for the majority of us.

Eventually, a hybrid approach of working virtually on some days and face-to-face on others may become the reality within many organizations. Leaders who adapt quickly, are innovative, and learn new ways to stay in touch and engage with their teams have the potential for a major win-win. Adaptability has definitely become the new currency. Welcome to the future.

"Giving employees great autonomy and flexibility allows people to feel independent and empowered while still feeling like a part of something bigger. This leads to happy, loyal employees with a rich quality of life, which in turn leads to an amazing culture."

—Larry English

"Multicultural leadership is the ability of those in managerial or leadership roles to recognize and understand how cultural backgrounds may affect a person's mindset, expectations, and work performance in different situations."

Chapter Six

MULTICULTURAL LEADERSHIP

Having grown up in one of the most culturally diverse cities in the United States, I had the benefit of broad exposure to many different cultures and ethnicities. I have always believed that experience is an asset to me.

Multicultural leadership is the ability of those in managerial or leadership roles to recognize and understand how cultural backgrounds may affect a person's mindset, expectations, and work performance in different situations. With this awareness, leaders are more adaptive and curious and have an open attitude toward other cultures. My message to multicultural leaders is to honor, accept, and understand that you make a difference to all employees you serve, especially those in your cultural group. Multiculturalism is here to stay. The success of an organization's diversity and inclusion efforts are in the hands of leadership at all levels. Leaders must lead by example, and not just talk about it, but be about it.

Individuals in positions of power influence attitudes, break stereotypes, and are role models for others who aspire to be in a leadership role in their organization.

Several nuances of multicultural leadership may be intuitively recognized, but not openly discussed, such as expectations of employees, expectations of different cultural groups, and the expected respect for the diversity of the people you serve. There is an expectation that you see them, take an interest in their success, and understand some of the challenges they may face as they navigate their course in the corporate environment. Many can benefit from mentorship or sponsorship, depending on their career aspirations.

Through leadership development initiatives, organizations can enhance the growth and mindset of their leaders as they relate to diversity and inclusion. In doing so, they will create leaders that are more receptive, intentional, and open-minded when collaborating with team members of diverse cultural backgrounds. One of the things I believe about multiculturalism is that inclusion should not only be an invitation to have a seat at the table, but also an opportunity to have a voice and be heard. Leaders must understand, respect, and accept it as a social responsibility to those they serve.

As a leader, I personally made it a best practice to be welcoming, approachable, accessible, and supportive. My team became a model of the same approach. Each one, teach one, as the saying goes.

Representation matters and has a significant effect.
For many individuals, seeing someone like yourself attain a high position can be the inspiration needed to pursue a similar path. There have been countless occasions when multicultural associates expressed their appreciation for my presence and leadership style. It meant a lot to them to have a woman of color lead a team of high-caliber professionals. When I experienced those moments, I was humbled and felt a great responsibility to exceed their expectations.

Honoring the diverse and unique backgrounds of the people I served was rewarding in many ways. Taking the time to listen while they shared their story meant a great deal to them. It also meant a lot that they trusted me enough to take the risk to share and be vulnerable. Building bridges of common understanding enabled us to collaborate effectively and really do some great work. Even though many years have transpired, there is still a bond that continues to keep us connected and in touch via social media, text messages, and phone calls.

***

I worked with several leaders who had a deep understanding and appreciation for the value of diversity and inclusion before it became a "thing" that was widely promoted and supported by many organizations. These leaders displayed respect, curiosity, and caring. This spoke to who those leaders really were when no one was watching. It spoke to their integrity. I can honestly say it was a privilege and pleasure to have served as a member of their leadership team.

I have benefitted greatly from working with leaders who took an interest in my success. It meant a lot when Mike D. showed interest and devoted his time to support me. When I received the Small Business Administration's Business Person of the Year Award, Mike was there. When I was recognized in the *Des Moines Register's* Up & Comers annual spotlight on local leaders and businesspeople, Mike was there. When I was featured as A Person Making a Difference by a local news station, Mike was there. Having his support and interest in me as a person left a lasting impression and became the leadership template to follow for many years to come.

Mike's leadership was very thoughtful and insightful. He seemed to intuitively understand the importance of his role in assisting others to open their minds to diversity and inclusion. There was an incident where a racial comment was made during one of our company meetings. Mike did not try to minimize the comment. He addressed it immediately with the individual. Furthermore, with the intention of helping his sales team build stronger relationships, Mike sponsored dinners at his home for the purpose of bringing together couples of diverse backgrounds.

Without Mike's leadership around our multicultural reality, getting to know the other team members would not have happened as easily. When I look back, it puts a smile on my face to recall the richness of our shared experiences as a result of those Friday dinners at Mike's home. I have to say, thank you, Mike, for having the leadership courage to stand on principle.

I had the great fortune of making a connection with another executive leader who I actually didn't work with directly, but I had exposure to by way of the work we both did. This is the other Mike (Mike K.) that entered my professional life. At company meetings, I observed how this Mike interacted with other executives and with his diverse sales team. It was well known that he led one of the highest-performing sales teams in the company. This was reminiscent of the experience I had with the first Mike earlier in my career.

Mike always seemed to make the time to connect with me at meetings and company events. This was not always the case with other leaders. Many of them seemed preoccupied with other individuals they may have deemed more important. Over the years, our conversations became richer as we shared perspectives on the business and personal outlooks on life events. I considered Mike to be an informal mentor. As time went on, he would ask about my career aspirations and encouraged me to expand my view of opportunities in the market area. The more I learned about Mike, the more I wanted to be a member of his team. I knew I'd learn a lot from being under his leadership.

Mike had been challenging me to consider a different career path than the one I was on at the time. He'd often say, "Janette, based on your experience and expertise, you have got to be getting bored with what you're currently doing." Well, Mike was definitely on point with that observation because earlier that year, I had decided to channel my energy and time into researching, planning, and then launching Fit & Fabulous – A Fitness Studio for Women as a side hustle to my nine-to-five. I thoroughly enjoyed the creative process and my return to entrepreneurship. The challenge of working in both spaces fulfilled me. So, with Mike's encouragement, I decided to interview for a position that would have landed me on his team. But as fate would have it, Mike was appointed to another leadership position shortly after I was selected. Despite this, Mike and I continued to keep in touch over the years periodically.

***

Amid the Covid-19 pandemic, America got another wake-up call that amplified intense discussions about the Black Lives Matter (BLM) movement and racial injustice realities. Organizations here and abroad were dealing with concerns of company employees and customer expectations, and the stakes were high for all. As the BLM movement continued to unfold, at first state-by-state, then country-by-country, several leaders from my company, the local community, and business associates from my circle of influence began to reach out to me to initiate conversation. Most reached out to express their support or gain a better perspective and understanding of "the Black experience."

So here we are, the entire world has been turned inside out with social injustice protests and the BLM movement. More than fifteen years had passed since Mike K. and I first met. And who did I hear from? Yes, you guessed it, Mike. At a time he knew was unsettling for all of us, but especially for a person of color, Mike reached out to see how all of it was impacting me. As he shared during our exchange, "Hope needs to turn to action, and action to results." Our conversation ended with Mike saying, "Friends don't have colors; they're just friends." My relationship with Mike has definitely gone beyond mentorship and has evolved into an authentic friendship. Though we don't talk often, whenever we do, the conversations are always very rich.

I had countless conversations about the turn of events with other business partners and leaders. What many thought they understood was quickly exposed as superficial and merely scratching the surface. However, what stood out was the transparency and vulnerability these leaders displayed at a time when expectations were high. There was no doubt in my mind that their response to the events as they were unfolding was in full view, and everyone was watching.

Such was the case with a company that had me as a client. Over the years we worked together, we had developed a strong business and personal relationship. So after the events unfolded and elevated the BLM movement discussions, the firm's managing partners earnestly reached out to me. Both partners were very forthcoming and vulnerable as they opened up about their insecurities around race relations. They knew there were expectations for them to respond and address what was happening, but they were uncertain about how best to approach it.

We agreed to a Zoom meeting, and at that meeting, we discussed their concerns, responsibility to their employees, clients, and the community they serve. I clarified misconceptions on several issues and shed light on others from my point of view. I offered strategies to foster understanding and support for their diverse team and clients, as well as ideas on how to pay it forward within the community. They expressed gratitude for the time we spent together. Though I wasn't quite sure of the actions they were committed to taking, I was certain our conversation elevated their understanding. I had faith that once they sorted things out, they would take the appropriate next steps.

Less than a week later, I was humbled by the thank-you letter I received and a summary of the actions they took to address diversity and inclusion realities at their firm. Additionally, they included a plan to promote financial literacy in their community. This represents an example of an organization taking ownership of its commitment to support diversity and inclusion within its organization and community. To Mike K.'s point, hope is not a plan. Hope needs to turn to action, and action to results.

"My dream would be a multicultural society, one that is diverse and where every man, woman and child are treated equally. I dream of a world where all people of all races work together in harmony."
—*Nelson Mandela*

"Even though leaders can adopt a leadership style that works best for them, thought should be given to how that style will impact the team and ultimately the work environment."

Chapter Seven

HOW ARE YOU SHOWING UP?

Self-awareness of how you show up is critical, especially when it involves and impacts the people around you. Reminiscent of the folktale "The Emperor's New Clothes" by Hans Christian Anderson, I've had my share of leaders who believe their own hype. Those of us who are consciously aware always pick up on what the real deal is. During many of those times we had to have a sense of humor just get through it all. Unfortunately, we have to put up with this nonsense until a line is drawn in the sand. Some things are, what they are.

A member of my team made an observation during one of our meetings with a leader that motivated him to send me a note. Here is what the note said:

> I wish that I had a perfect thing to say, to make everything okay. I don't, but here are some thoughts. The only way to help someone who is

low in self-awareness is with grace, patience, persistence, and truth. The only way to combat an atmosphere of posturing and image-consciousness is authenticity. You have too much to offer to the people who need you, to give in or give up. That does not mean that it will be easy or over soon. There will be more ups and downs. But there also could be beauty and growth. I believe in you.

I was surprised and touched by the note and appreciated this team member's level of awareness and compassion.

Obviously, this leader brought a different energy into our office whenever she visited. My team member intuitively discerned the differences between me and this leader and the way we internalized and projected our personas.

Fortunately, I understood who I was dealing with. Knowing that an egocentric mindset can get in the way and obscure even the best of intentions, I allowed her to have the stage and do her thing. In contrast, I resolved to maintain the commitment to my style of leadership—leading with authenticity and self-awareness and remaining focused on meeting the needs of my team. It was a teachable moment for everyone.

I learned a long time ago that developing a sense of humor can be important, although I know this is not a laughing matter at all. One of my former colleagues likened working with his manager to getting a root canal. Anticipating a root canal and having the actual procedure done is definitely not my idea of fun. Simply put, you just want to get the darn thing over and done with.

When I heard his experience described that way, I was disappointed. I thought to myself, "If this is how his manager is showing up, what a pitiful state of affairs. He deserved so much more." Although not all employees experience leaders in the same manner, it is important to acknowledge that there is probably a basis for his perception of the situation. From my view, this leader's pattern of behavior was obviously not a one-time occurrence. It's feasible to discern that most of their interactions up to that point comprised the basis for this employee's outlook. And I would guess many others on the team would agree as they interacted with this same manager. A root canal? Damn!

***

After thirty years of observation and personal experience, I have concluded that there's no single optimal way to be an effective leader. There's not one leadership style that works best or perfectly in every situation. To determine which of the leadership styles may be right for the results desired, you may want to consider a few different factors.

- What situation are you facing?
- What's the best leadership style for the situation?
- Which approach is the best fit for your team?
- What's the expected outcome?

Even though leaders can adopt a leadership style that works best for them, thought should be given to how that style will impact the team and ultimately the work environment. All leaders need to know and internalize this because they are responsible for the energy generated by how they show up for their team. Either positive and motivating or the complete opposite, your team will respond accordingly. When you have a talented team, their expectations of you are high. They expect as much from you as you expect from them. As mentioned before, leadership goes both ways. When you respect and value your team, that alone will determine how you show up, and your team knows that.

I encountered many different leadership styles during my professional journey. The majority of my experiences with leaders were exceptional. Some were visionaries with the ability to inspire us to rally around specific business goals; a few others were team-focused and provided a myriad of resources; and many were collaborative, allowing an opportunity for everyone to have a voice. Then there were the leaders that were stuck in their ways who attempted to hold everyone to seemingly prescriptive standards without even considering other more effective leadership styles.

You might identify with one or more of the leadership styles below. If you aspire to become a better or a blissful leader, do an honest self-check to determine where you are on the leadership spectrum.

Transformational Leadership
Transformational leaders work with the goal of transforming their teams so that they are constantly improving. They create a vision of the future that they share with their teams so everyone can work together toward that goal. Transformational leaders are also often seen as authentic, self-aware, and empathetic. They handle conflict amongst team members effectively by holding their team members as well as themselves accountable for resolution and a positive outcome.

Servant Leadership

Servant leaders work hard to meet the needs of their team. They are often seen as charismatic, collaborative, and generous. This often leads to high worker satisfaction since team members feel heard and cared for in the work they do. It can also be beneficial in a working environment where you want everyone to see themselves as equals who are working together on an even playing field, rather than focusing on who is in charge of whom.

Democratic Leadership

Democratic leaders include their team members in their decision-making process. While they are ultimately responsible for making final decisions, they often ask team members what they think and try to take their thoughts and opinions into account, which helps increase engagement. This is an effective leadership style if you have your team members' trust and know that they are experienced, do exceptional work, and leverage their resources and time well.

Transactional Leadership

Transactional leadership focuses on the idea that accepting a job is a transaction. The individual is less important than the job that needs to be done. This style can seem cold or inflexible and may lead to low job satisfaction for team members who want to be recognized for their skill sets and the experience they have.

Bureaucratic Leadership

Bureaucratic leaders are all about rules. They may set strict procedures that they follow precisely, and they expect their team to do the same. This usually is not the best leadership style for teams that rely on innovation or creative problem-solving. This leadership style could be a good fit in those situations where team members have an appreciation for a very cut-and-dried set of rules and procedures to follow so they are not left guessing about what is expected of them.

I have had my share of transactional and bureaucratic leaders at various times during my career. I have experienced and witnessed how those approaches can demotivate you by creating an unrewarding and highly stressful work environment. Like "helicopter parents," leaders who hover or micromanage create a dynamic that stifles relationships, crushes optimism, frustrates employees, and dampens their enthusiasm to do their best work. I found that leaders with these tendencies are uninspiring, challenging, and hard to even connect with. Their insistence on the only and perfect solution to almost every business issue overlooks the value and opportunity for collaboration, creative problem-solving, and building trust. I have several memories of those times, but none of them are fond ones.

In contrast, my main focus and approaches were on fostering a healthier environment where my team would be engaged, challenged in a productive way, and primed to perform at their best. In my role as manager, as members of my team demonstrated the proper level of understanding and competence based on their experience or training, I supported them with greater levels of independence. Even if a team member had not done a specific task before, if they were confident, willing to try, and demonstrated the desire to succeed, my approach was to let them pursue it. There's no doubt that being directive has its time and place during the developmental process. However, assessing your team's capabilities before swooping in is a more effective approach.

Ultimately, when employees are micromanaged, they become frustrated, which stunts their desire to be innovative, creative, and productive. I have to say, swooping in was never my approach. My primary motivation was for everyone on the team to find the everyday joy in the work and relationships that occupied such a significant amount of their time, energy, and focus. Who wants to be miserable 24/7? I certainly didn't, and neither did my team.

So change your approach, and you will soon discover the talents your team has as well as uncover areas of opportunities to collaborate with them. As a leader, the ways I supported my team encompassed being accessible, being a resource or sounding board, and communicating with them frequently without obsessing over every detail of their work assignments.

How leaders show up for their team at critical times can influence their team's perception of them. Recently, an employee shared that he suffered two personal losses within days of each other. In light of his situation, as well as decisions and arrangements he needed to make to be there for his family, the employee expected the manager to focus on the situation and have the confidence to provide support in that moment. Rather than displaying leadership and showing compassion, this manager's decision was to lean into policies and procedures instead of putting the employee first and then handling any administrative details on the back end. This was a missed opportunity to show up and demonstrate effective leadership by supporting this employee in a way that made him feel respected, valued, and protected. As might be expected, the employee was disappointed with his manager's lack of emotional intelligence and, in his eyes, lack of leadership ability given the situation. Whether or not this employee's perception is an accurate assessment of his manager's abilities, it certainly did reshaped his outlook of their relationship.

I have deep respect for leaders who are confident in who they are and make everyone feel like they matter and are important to the overall goals of the organization. However, many individuals are all about their title, authority, and rank. I observed this phenomenon many times in my career and made it a point never to emulate it. Several years ago, I worked with a newly appointed leader who spent most of the time talking about himself and his agenda, which bored everyone else to tears. He was surprised when the team didn't engage with him at the level he expected and ultimately wanted. Eventually, he did gain awareness, but there was a lot of time wasted in the interim, and as a result a bit of his credibility was lost. We had higher expectations of him. Despite his shortcomings, we gave him the grace and space to grow into the position by modeling what team engagement really looks like. Over time he became less anxious, more comfortable with asking thought-provoking questions, a better listener, and more open to ideas from the team.

***

The opportunity to serve as a blissful leader as well as a transformational coach took place with my interactions with a former colleague. When I first met him, he was on a different team, and since we had similar professional backgrounds and experiences, it was inevitable that our paths would cross. When they did, he would incessantly relive an unhappy period in his career, not only to me but to anyone who would listen. In some ways, I believe he told that story because he thought he had something to prove. It was his opportunity to express dissatisfaction with the direction of his career at that time. As a result, he overshadowed the brilliant person he actually was, which caused others to have a skewed perception of him. However, I looked beyond all of that, recognized the attributes that could qualify him for a leadership position, and decided to coach him on letting his light shine.

Prior to joining my team, we would have informal conversations about his career, his aspirations, and the value of changing his mindset. If he wanted to make progress, he had to change that narrative and speak more life into his present and future. In the course of those exchanges, we both agreed that it was counterproductive to continue with the same old story. I slowly began to work with him on his mindset, and the tone of his conversations became more optimistic. With less talk about the past, he recognized that his future was brighter than he had originally perceived.

Two years later, he was assigned to my team, which created an opportunity to work with him directly. We collaborated on vision, mission, and aspirations for the future as they related to his professional and personal goals. While a member of my team, he became recognized as one of my highest performers. In addition to frequent coaching conversations, I demonstrated my trust, support, and confidence by increased levels of responsibility and recommending him for special projects whenever the opportunity presented itself. His contributions were impressive as he showcased his genius. Transformation into an influential, valued, and positive team member was recognized and led to his selection for a position on the leadership team. Mission accomplished!

"Leadership is communicating to people their worth and potential, so clearly they come to see it in themselves."

—Stephen R. Covey

Conclusion

Blissful Leadership is the culmination of three decades of wisdom gained through introspection, observation, experience, and practice. In retrospect, I am awestruck by the caliber of people I was privileged to work with, the developmental opportunities afforded me, and the exposure I received during all of those years. Much like a kaleidoscope, my career has been diverse, colorful, and multidimensional. Each emerging and unique experience symbolized opportunities for fresh perspectives, insights, and personal growth.

To paraphrase Alice Walker, "When there are no models available to emulate, one must become the model." Becoming the model and having the confidence to show up as myself empowered me to move from success to significance in business as well as in my personal life. There is purpose in achieving balance as a blissful leader. It creates an imprint and enhances the overall experience not only for yourself but also all the people you encounter and serve.

I reached a point in my career when I knew my work was done. I made a choice to set my vision forward and turn the final page of this chapter. In doing this, launching my next chapter was an easier decision than I expected. Being time-rich, I can now fully embrace the lifestyle I envisioned: being of sound body and mind, experience the joy, peace, and freedom of being at home, creating memories with family and friends, meeting with my clients, and of course, spending time with my beloved Jadabear.

"It's a new dawn. It's a new day. It's a new life for me and I'm feeling good!"
—Nina Simone

Janette Blissett
Next Chapter Experience, LLC

The act of balancing stones carries with it a practice of patience and a physical effort of creating balance.

BLISSFUL REFLECTIONS
WRITE DOWN YOUR THOUGHTS

BLISSFUL REFLECTIONS
WRITE DOWN YOUR THOUGHTS

BLISSFUL REFLECTIONS
WRITE DOWN YOUR THOUGHTS

BLISSFUL REFLECTIONS
WRITE DOWN YOUR THOUGHTS

BLISSFUL REFLECTIONS
WRITE DOWN YOUR THOUGHTS